What The Truth Tastes Like

second edition

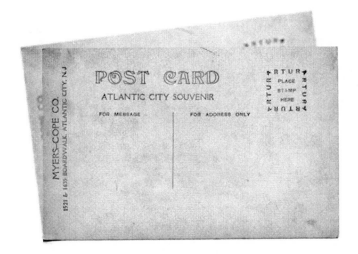

Martha Silano

Two Sylvias Press

Two Sylvias Press
PO Box 1524
Kingston, WA 98346
twosylviaspress@gmail.com

Cover Design: Kelli Russell Agodon
Book Design: Annette Spaulding-Convy
Author Photo: Langdon Cook

Created with the belief that *great writing is good for the world*, Two Sylvias Press mixes modern technology, classic style, and literary intellect with an eco-friendly heart. We draw our inspiration from the poetic literary talent of Sylvia Plath and the editorial business sense of Sylvia Beach. We are an independent press dedicated to publishing the exceptional voices of writers.

For more information about Two Sylvias Press or to learn more about the eBook version of *What The Truth Tastes Like* please visit: www.twosylviaspress.com

What The Truth Tastes Like (First Edition) was published by Nightshade Press, 1999.

Second Edition. Created in the United States of America.

ISBN-13: 978-0692379783

ISBN-10: 0692379789

Two Sylvias Press
www.twosylviaspress.com

Praise For *What The Truth Tastes Like*

Martha Silano reveals that she *invented the perpetually grieving Linzer torte and the self-effervescing catbox lid* and I believe her. Her poems are full of good stuff—sausages and Oklahoma villages and dreams of parrots. Even when love has gone sour and the lover has gone south, the energy and inventiveness never flag. We know she'll be right back, offering more truthful tastes. Take a big bite, this is a strong first serving.
–Robert Hershon

ജ

Martha Silano writes with wit and intelligence, and she is equally at home naming the birds on a beach and the arcana of the yellow pages. It is her love of language that distinguishes these poems and makes them so full of startling awareness, and this not only at the level of the word, but also in the syntax, which reveals the mind's continual approach and avoidance of its emotional home.
–Alison Hawthorne Deming

ജ

The truth tastes like these succulent poems. Their refrains will form on your lips and ring in your heart. In these rich, elegant--and wickedly witty--pieces, Martha Silano has captured the rhythms that percolate, unheard by the rest of us, just beneath the surface of everyday life.
–Laura Kalpakian

ജ

From clear-eyed attention to the ordinary world, Martha Silano makes poems that instruct, startle, and give pleasure as only a great poem can.
–David Kirby

Acknowledgements

Grateful acknowledgement is given to the editors of the following magazines in which these poems, some in earlier versions, first appeared:

Angle: "A Stalk Of Winterberries" and "At The Hoot 'N Holler Guest House In Uncertain, Texas"

Artful Dodge: "They're Prohibited By City Ordinance" and "In Nature One Seldom Sees Circles"

Cascadia Review: "Ode To Olfactory" and "I Dream A Kind Of Peace"

City Lit Rag: "Self-Portrait In The Studio" and "He Was Not Contagious"

Crab Creek Review: "In Henry Carlile's *Writing 213*"

Escape Into Life: "Control Top Panty" and "Schadenfreude"

Filter: "Page Turners"

The Florida Review: "The Tables Of Losses" (rpt. in *Switched-on Gutenberg*)

Green Mountains Review: "My Hour With Jorie Graham"

Hanging Loose: "When You Didn't Call" and "Such A Way To Go"

Hubbub: "Winter: Early Evening"

Jeopardy: "The Man Who Slept In My Bed" and "Ladybug"

LitRag: "Holly Hock Bakery's Moving To Madison Valley"

Paris Review: "What I Meant To Say Before I Said "'So Long'""

Poemeleon: "What's Free" and "Because I Am Fully Conversant With My Hideous Qualities"

Poetry Northwest: "For A Friend Who'd Prefer A Sestina," "For A Friend Who Sends Me A Flyer On The Art Of Ear Candling And News Her Book Has Arrived," "Just Don't Write Any Poems About Niagara Falls," "A Trip Through The Yellow Pages: Ba, Be, And So Forth," "The Sausage Parade," "Spellcheck Changes *Silano* To *Saline*," "The Moon," and "Response To A Letter From My Ex"

Potato Eyes: "To The Woman Who, When I Went To Heat My Pizza In The Office Microwave, Asked Me Who Are *You*?" "Sweet Red Peppers, Sun-Drieds, The Hearts Of Artichokes," and "Men Of The Stone Age Had No Use For Fractions"

Prairie Schooner: "This Is Not An Envy Poem"

Rattle: "What The Grad Students Said"

Thrush: "Do Not Touch The Art"

Truck: "Full Tilt" and "The Miracles Of Jesus"

Verse: "Shrimp Arithmetic"

Gracious thanks to the Millay Colony for the Arts, the University of Arizona Poetry Center, Dorland Mountain Arts Colony, and the Virginia Center for the Creative Arts for much needed time, solitude, and generous financial support.

"When You Didn't Call," "To The Woman Who, When I Went To Heat My Pizza In The Office Microwave, Asked Me Who Are *You*?" and "Such A Way To Go" appear in *Pontoon: An Anthology of Washington State Poets.*

"The Sausage Parade" appeared on *Poetry Daily,* January 27, 2000.

"In Henry Carlile's *Writing 213,*" "The Moon," "Such A Way To Go," and "To The Woman Who, When I Went To Heat My Pizza In The Office Microwave, Asked Me Who Are *You*?" appear in *American Poetry: The Next Generation*, Jim Daniels and Gerald Costanzo, Eds. (Carnegie Mellon U. Press, 2000).

"The Sausage Parade" appears in *Poetry Daily: 366 Poems from the World's Most Popular Poetry Website,* Diane Boller, Don Selby, Chryss Yost, Eds. (Sourcebooks, 2003).

"Sweet Red Peppers, Sun-Drieds, The Hearts Of Artichokes" appears in *O Taste and See: Poems About Food*, David Lee Garrison and Terry Hermsen, Eds. (Bottom Dog Press, 2003).

"At The Shorebird Festival: Grays Harbor County, Washington" appears in *Birds in the Hand: Fiction and Poetry About Birds,* Kent Nelson and Dylan Nelson, Eds. (Farrar, Straus, and Giroux, 2004).

"The Sausage Parade" appears in *Seriously Funny: Poems about Love, Death, Religion, Art, Politics, Sex, and Everything Else,* Barbara Hamby and David Kirby, Eds. (University of Georgia Press, 2010).

Sincerest gratitude to Molly Tenenbaum, Dina Ben-Lev, Stacey Luftig, Debra Elfenbein, Michele Glazer, David Wagoner, Heather McHugh, Dirk Stratton, Eleanor Hamilton, John W. Marshall, Kim Mackay, and Marie & Alfred Silano.

This book is for Langdon Cook.

Table of Contents

III. What The Truth Tastes Like

The Ladybug's Way: On The Poems Of Martha Silano

It's impossible not to love a poem with a title like "Because I Am Fully Conversant with My Hideous Qualities," just as you can't help falling for the poet who wrote it.

And as with any other romance, engagement at a gut level is essential as both players step onto the tennis court of love to swat the ball back and forth. Thwack! Surely you can't be as awful as you say you are, you say. Pow—oh, yes, I am! No, no, you cry, let me tell you—ungh!—about my own shortcomings.

And so the game goes till the end, till writer and reader lie sweat-drenched in each other's arms.

Actually, list poems are rather a specialty of Martha Silano. Take "Letter from Here," which is her version of the poem we've all written (at least in our minds) to our classmates of yore—in Martha's case, to everybody from Jamie Feltovic and the D'Alfonsi twins to Bobby Westowksi. You remember them, don't you? Of course, you do. You, too, went to school with those kids, even though they had different names.

Her true list-poem triumph, though, is "In the Self-Help Aisle," in which she manages to shoehorn 18 self-help titles into a 16 short lines. As soon as you read

> she had *Mixed Feelings*, but she knew *What You Feel You Can Heal,,*
> so she decided it was time to *Find a Husband at 35 . . . ,*

you think, why didn't I write this poem myself?

But by the time you finish, you realize that Martha Silano did a better job with this topic than any of the rest of us could. Oh, and there are actually 19 book titles in the poem, since its lovelorn protagonist spies a gent with his nose in Darwin's *Voyage of the Beagle*.

Speaking of evolution. . . .

Actually, Silano's poems are an argument against evolution, at least in the sense that they advocate a sort of benign literal-mindedness in place of the overheated razzle-dazzle that many a poetic striver has pursued to his or her peril.

No, Silano leaps miles by taking a step backward and bringing to the world a true sense of wonder, as in "Joy," an ode to, not that feeling of pleasure described by German poet Friedrich Schiller and then immortalized musically by

Ludwig van Beethoven in the final movement of his Ninth Symphony, but the best-selling-because-highly-effective dishwashing liquid manufactured by the Procter & Gamble corporation.

Similarly, when this poet is betrayed by computer software, does she throw herself on the floor and sob as the rest of us do? No, she whips up a tangy lemonade from the lemons handed to her by Bill Gates and his minions. The result is a poem called "Spellcheck Changes *Silano* to *Saline*," whose first line begins, "but I don't mind. . . ."

See what literal-mindedness can do for you, you poets? Spellcheck changes "Kirby" to "choirboy" all the time, but until now, it never occurred to me to embrace that flub-up, to take it at face value and let it lead me through the literal world to one of breathtaking loveliness, a world festooned, at the poem's end, in "sticky daisy, / sand verbena, / rocket pea, bill of the pirouetting phalarope."

What I call benign literal-mindedness has produced great poems for millennia. Where would poetry be if Keats had walked right past that dusty Greek vase in the British Museum or said, "Stupid bird!" when the nightingale sang to him? What if Emily Dickinson had swatted the "narrow fellow in the grass" with a garden hoe, if Whitman hadn't looked at himself in the mirror and thought, "Hmm, I can get a poem out of this"?

III

In "Ladybug," Silano outlines her *ars poetica* in a deceptively simple way. In fact, the whole *ars* is in the first three lines, which read, "When she reaches the end / Of a shoe or a table, she keeps / Walking." Is that not what poets do? They approach this world with no more agenda than the ladybug has, enumerating its tragedies and joys. The best poets show us the surprises we'd miss out on otherwise, and you can't be surprised if you've already made up your mind.

Mainly, the best poets show us the world's beauties, and you'll find no more beautiful poem in a book out there today than "When You Didn't Call." As its title suggests, here Silano is writing about heartbreak, and in heartbreak she locates something more beautiful than any painting, any Bach suite spooling out of a cello. Our emotional life is "black like a starling," says the speaker, but it's also "white like a flowering hawthorn."

From clear-eyed attention to the ordinary world, Martha Silano makes poems that instruct, startle, and give pleasure as only a great poem can.

David Kirby

I. THE SAUSAGE PARADE

THE MAN WHO SLEPT IN MY BED

is somewhere over Oklahoma: Broken
Arrow, Shamrock, Marble City.

By now he's bugged the stewardess twice
for scotch and soda, the latest

Cowboys/Redskins score. If he isn't asleep,
if he's near a window, he's looking down

on Scraper, Nebo, Joy. And when the honey-roasted
peanuts make the rounds: Bromide, Mustang, Homer.

Tries to read and his mind drifts off.
Dreams of open spaces, grey birds

with scissor tails, what it might be like to border
Texas, come equipped with a handle.

The captain announces the final score
as the plane glides over Wapanucka,

Freedom, Comanche, Strong, and I'm
in my bedroom, eyes glued

to the lower left-hand corner, ten miles west
of Friendship, to the town of Martha.

*Why do you have a map of Oklahoma
on your wall?* he asked the night he left.

I could sooner explain Orion, Wheeless,
Eagle City, I could sooner explain Love

County, or the South Canadian River.
He's somewhere over Oklahoma

circling Crystal, Hollis, Lone Grove.
He doesn't even think of me at Boiling

Springs, Ringling, Purdy, Loco,
doesn't know there's an Okay, a Loyal,

a Mutual. Doesn't know we could settle down
in Sweet Water, raise a family in Muse,

can't imagine growing old in Sugarville
or camped in the Winding Stair Mountains.

He's somewhere over Oklahoma, not over me.

LADYBUG

When she reaches the end
Of a shoe or a table, she keeps
Walking. If she needs the help of wings,
Wings appear. If she lands on her back,
Her hind legs find the world and turn her
Over. When the wings forget to fold,
They drag like a slip from a scarlet dress.

Where did this one in my kitchen come from?
Did a neighbor, in a fit of aphid rage,
Release a thousand? Is this a sign?
Am I to count the spots?

Time Teller, Child Bringer,
Pursuer of Missing Sheep:
What will be next?
Predacious diving beetles?
Scarabs named Goliath?
Bombardiers that shoot a puff of gas?
Don't uninvited guests bring relatives?

But God's Almighty Cow,
Marienkäfer and Kin to Hen and Dove,
How can I kick you out?

Girls put you on the tips of their fingers.
Where you fly they'll meet a spouse.
Cousin to Whirligig, Sharer of Parts
With the Snouted Weevil, is this the home
Where you thought you'd find
Your children? Whoever sang to you lied.

WHEN YOU DIDN'T CALL

I listened to a woman on the bus (*three billion
heartbeats equal a lifetime*). I fell in love
with Puccini, every *isole*, every high-pitched

wail. In a drugstore a man approached me, holding
a bottle: *Is this for the hair?*
What confused him were the words *builds body.*

I can't believe it, I barely heard, beneath
my bedroom window. You didn't call
and I reached for my Magic 8-Ball. All

it could say? *Try again later.* It poured. It poured
and got colder. A flock of birds
squeaked in a tree. I dreamed

of a high place, miles of granite.
We are like that, I thought, black like a starling,
white like a flowering hawthorn.

POSTCARDS FROM ALTEA, SPAIN

1.

We're our usual, conglomerate selves. My hair's
a sickly green (the pool in Madrid), J's only decent
shirt got doused with extra-virgin. We're still
overestimating portions, which only half explains
our nightly game of rice ball toss. Cherries
are down to four hundred pesetas a kilo:
guess what we've been spitting off the terrace?

2.

Today at the store I couldn't remember the word
for onion. The clerk held up an eggplant. When
I shook my head, she reached for a bunch of garlic.
She looked so certain: how could I tell her?

3.

We've started noticing things. Piles of abandoned
rocks. Wires that go nowhere. The lemons I stole
from a scraggly tree: thick and juiceless.

4.

Tonight we played Hit the Antifreeze Jug with a Sneaker.
From ten till four La Discoteca shook our mosquito coils.

5.

I miss home—American coffee. J wants to return
to Barcelona, but one encounter with Chamy
(the razor-munching fakir) was enough for me.
Did I tell you I saw a beggar scrape ice cream
from the cracks in a sidewalk?

6.

It's our last day so we're blanching beans.
J dreams of cushioned toilet seats. My mind's
simpler, drifts to stacks of Charmin Ultra Soft.
We'll call when we get in.

she had *Mixed Feelings*, but she knew *What You Feel You Can Heal*,
so she decided it was time to *Find a Husband at 35*. He was sitting

in Nature & Outdoors, an excellent specimen. *Sex, Money, and Power*,
she thought, but first she needed to thumb through *Exhibitionism*

for the Shy, get past her *Shining Affliction*, consider *Men, Women,
and Relationships*. This could take awhile, but if she focused on

The Art of Thinking, this *Sleepwalker Wakening* might not have to
Migrate to Solitude to win her affections. Then she spied it—

the telltale wedding band. So that's why he paid no mind!
He must know *The Secrets of a Very Good Marriage,*

Finding the Love, but then again any second he could reach
above her, loosen *The Good Divorce* from between the clutches

of *Emotional Unavailability* and *The Transformative Power
of Crisis*. But no, he seemed happy enough with his nose inside

The Voyage of the Beagle, which gave her the chance to settle into *Joy
in the Everyday, Making Peace with Yourself, Composting a Life.*

CONTROL TOP PANTY

or should I say Waistnipper? Shaping skort? Barely-there
brief? When did we say we wanted control? When did we say

we wanted scallop-trimmed leg bands providing
generous coverage, all-day ease? The moon controls

the tides, the sun and rain, voluptuous tulips,
and now the Sassybax Torso Trimmer,

like a Schlackwurst casing, our 21st century curves.
Is this a shapewear revolution, a tucking

and smoothing manifesto, a binding-digging-poking
overthrow, advanced construction equaling

all our foremothers marched for, antithesis
of undergarments singed? But these high power

panties, these impeccably smoothing Spanx,
speak nothing of sweeping change, of overturn

and upset—of nothing radically catastrophic,
of nothing breaking down. No longer letting it all

hang out, no longer bothered by bonding, still we long
for groundbreaking comfort, comfort while shrinking

two sizes. Not only who holds the remote, who's closest
to the switch, but who turns the ignition, sparks the explosive,

sends the bodies hurling through the streets. (Don't
we all long to be the one with a finger in every pots

de crème?) Turn back, turn back we hear you saying;
you've forgotten all we fought for, the smallest toes broken,

bathed in a mixture of urine and blood, bandages pulled to the heel,
the foot bound and rebound till it resembled a three-inch golden lotus.

Forgotten crinoline cages, corsets believed a medical must,
whale bone and steel deforming internal organs. But we don't

want to seem unseemly, reveal our sublimating gorge
on the bucket-sized and extra-buttered, the 78-ounce

Gulp, so we squeeze ourselves in, surrender our unsmoothness,
our voluptuous bottoms, till we can barely breathe.

THIS IS NOT AN ENVY POEM

but it wants your pedicured feet those shiny bits
like miniature Christmas tree bulbs

this poem wants your screened-in porch
and your swinging porch swing

wants your snaking-through-the-fence
tomato plant which somehow didn't die

in the first hard frost this poem wants
your trip to Southeast Asia and your trip

to Bhutan wants all the birds on your life list
even and especially the scarlet macaw that swooped

on your Monteverde Cloud Forest picnic
this poem wants your view your smooth

and hairless calves your dog walking
the hardwood floors this poem wants

your gas grill your reading glasses
your black plastic pond with year-round goldfish

wants the duckweed that keeps it from growing
dank this poem wants to be as tall as you

tall and with pom-pom sweaters big pink pom-poms
this poem won't stop scratching at your door

like a desperate needy goat this poem wants to eat up
all your leftovers pick clean your meaty greasy bones

SWEET RED PEPPERS, SUN-DRIEDS, THE HEARTS OF ARTICHOKES

Pagliacci Pizza wants me.
Lying in bed on a Sunday morning,

I could almost want them back.
The trick, a deliverer said,

is learning to hesitate. Not in the car
or walking to the door, but just

inside, when they're waiting
for change.

Or I could manage a bingo hall,
swirl behind glass at the Lusty Lady.

Once it was a cornfield,
sixteen hours a day in a moving cage, reaching

for tassels. I've picked cherries, scooped
pickles, sold knives and rakes and

rolls that fell to the floor, all
while my bosses took up flying.

Maybe Pagliacci's wouldn't be bad:
evenings, a car, the minor streets

of Queen Anne. And at the end
of my shift, I could settle in—eating

what got sent back.

CHAINSAW SAVVY

I haven't got,
but I know

the calculus of difference.
My preventative know-how's

shot, but beyond the conics,
among exterior angles, I've found

my inner division.
I don't have the tools

for limbing and bucking,
but forced oscillations lead

to no other solution
but to magnify my pyramids.

I've been distressed by faulty compression,
by my lack of sharpening basics,

but thanks to astronomical calculations
(my own, indeterminate powers),

I can confidently assert a theory
of continuous transformation.

My carburetor's kaput,
my fuel link's kinked,

every spark plug loose,
but my curves are of the first order,

and I know the power of roots.

FOR A FRIEND WHO'D PREFER A SESTINA

Or a poem in which all the significant moments
rhyme with Debra, so that when, for instance,
my speaker stands outside her childhood home,
I have her whisper *abracadabra*, and thirty years
unfold: a rotary mower, all the mulch a potato bug
could hope for, enough tomatoes to cover the block
in a film of marinara, billions of leaves from a failing
oak. She's even sent me words (*love, batter run, rain,
watch, fez*) and wants it full of innocent strangers
planting tulips. *What's the correlation between
a person's dress and how he dresses a burger?*
and I know what she wants so well I take notes
at the Ringside till half my cells are their sirloin.
(All I can say with complete conviction, after Tie-
Dyed Tee and Tweed Suit slop the ketchup, and
Florsheim and Clear-Heels skip it altogether,
is none.) She doesn't want pyrotechnics, a word
from the man who set fire to an aging McCrory's:
*Make it be about baseball—Bobby Thigpen
and Lenny Dykstra.* Debi, I'm sure it isn't love
that batters run to, or rain they watch as the longest fly
of the season curves foul. The day you find yourself at home
in your new-found Lambertville, let the feeling stretch
from the Delaware River to Puget Sound. Then walk
down Bridge in faux fur fez, charming a cobra,
all that struck you as coiled and circuitous gone.

THE TABLE OF LOSSES

Both hands, both feet, both eyes,
a life. For these I'd receive

the Principal Sum, though there'd
be limitations, forms to fill out.

If it wasn't ptomaines, bacterial infection,
a self-inflicted wound or a war (declared

or not), I'd be referred to the Table
of Benefits, Class III, page 2. $20,000.00

isn't much, certainly not for the tears
(if eyes were not among the members

lost), barely enough to cover your bones,
my breasts. Already I've dug a hole

and begun to fill it: shared *couchette*
on the train to Rome (asked *sposato?*

we beamed like newlyweds), hike
to Yokum Ridge (when the trail

gave way to ice and rock, you climbed,
I watched). I'm in Bishop's boat—the one

with all the rainbows—fireweed, sky-
rocket, Indian paintbrush. Red shorts.

Blue bandana. Perfect arc of your back.

HE WAS NOT CONTAGIOUS

whispered epics in her ear,
some kind of Gilgamesh,

and maybe she'd been a lock
of raped hair. He cried out

I've seen the best minds . . .
recitations flung like Frisbees

into the Friday-night air.
She'd never believed in anything

soup can or tap shoe bright. He craved
a tattoo singing *babaloo-babaloo*;

what she wanted no man or menu
could deduce. Orange-fringed, carpet-

remnant kitsch, he was her bonafide
dulces suenos, but it was *buenos*

noches for this made-from-scratch
kid. Back then, when grief

was a matter of disembarking,
of barking into your beer.

Back then, when he whispered
don't decide too early how many

zeroes follow a rational number,
don't overestimate the indivisible.

He was mercury staying put; she,
a pathogen, an unfortunate

tic. He was sand dollar, quartzite;
she, like Skylab, on the verge

of kersplash.

WINTER: EARLY EVENING

When I tell you an abundance of hair
is a sign of impending wealth,
when I tell you the bone from a dogfish

will cure your kidney stones,
when I say, in short, long
ears/long life,

know that three of anything
is a sign of distress,
know that my days are full

of questions, absent ex's,
emptiness. When I tell you three
nutmegs hung around

the neck will take away
your boils, and dreams of eggs
and muddy water equal

trouble, when I say *plenty*
of ladybugs, plenty
of hops, know it is cold

and the short day loses
light. I'm alone.
Three is not enough.

THE MOON

Though its map is drenched with watery names—
Lake of Dreams, Sea of Clouds, Bay of Dew—
the moon is waterless. Temperatures range
from three-hundred above to three-hundred below.
Rising 15,000 feet, the Apennines
stood up long before Galileo.

To sleep in the light of the moon is to weaken
your sight. The moon, the bushmen say,
is a man who angered the sun. Red because
Earth is in the way, *bloody* moons
portend catastrophe. To wax and wane
in Tierra del Fuego, the moon puts on and loses weight.

Evil, fickle, noble, ruler of Monday,
giver of dreams and home of broken vows,
mirror, silver candle, assembler of stars;
only astronauts have seen your dark, mysterious
side. Though in pictures it looks like more,
Aldrin's footprint didn't sink an inch.

Once, in Kansas, on a golf course white
with snow, I saw you through a telescope.
Your brightness sent Orion to bed. When a rock
arrived at the Trenton Museum, I skipped school
to stand in line. In the Wallowas and the Bitterroots,
through the lace of urban curtains, I've watched you rise.

O place of lunacy, wasted treasures, squandered
time. Confuser of noodles, poppy, sad guitar.
Think of oceans, think of the taste of tears.
What something far away can guide.

IN PRAISE OF BODY HAIR

Thanks to the fringe
on their feet, water shrews walk

on water. The grainless pelt
of the star-nosed mole permits ease

whether rolling backward or forward.
The enormous ears of the Townsend's bat

are smooth, but what good are ears without
a snuggle-up-comfortably body?

Gray squirrel's tail: rudder, blanket,
umbrella; hollow-haired polar bear:

prize-winning swimmer. A piliferous belly
redeems the armadillo.

You who are cirrose, hispid, fleecy,
whose five o'clock shadow

casts darkness long before noon—
Queen of Stubble, King of Tufts—

you who've been teased
for your papoose, bristles, fluff:

let crinosity embrace you,
your whiskers knowingly gauging the spaces

through which we all must pass.

JENNIFER'S PEACHES CARDINAL HUME FOR THE PRIESTS
    AT WESTMINSTER CATHEDRAL

Half the time a miracle
not blowing up the kitchen,
not having the seeds
of mustard or poppy spurt
from an oily pan
like so many curses unbidden
(why doesn't the recipe mention lids?);
the rest of the time *excuse me for cooking!*
but the seeds keep right on popping,
or the oven explodes in a Mephisthophelean
flash, smack dab in the middle
of fixing forty garlic chicken—
sixteen peeled, twenty-four to go.
O, my St. Margaret puff pastry
poofed. O, my Toad-in-the-Hole kaput.
Something's missing. And he, not
stopping to swallow before he speaks:
Flavor? Do you think it might be flavor?

THE MIRACLES OF JESUS

Pulled a coin from a fish's mouth, bought a lottery ticket
worth $666,000, fifty-two equal payments. Morphed

a few measly loaves into billions of breadcrumbs,
bottomless pan of Momma Shea's Best-Ever Meatloaf.

Turned Talking Rain into Chardonnay, Arrow Springs
into Pinot Grigio, all the while skittering over the sea

like a feisty Basilisk, all the while reviving Lazarus, ridding
the world of its bleeding and blindness, its leprous

and dropsied. *Get up and walk!* And crutches toppled
like tombstones while spirits and demons hightailed it

up the Jordan River. So many mackerel, the nets
unknotted, loosed from the fishermen's no longer

withered hands. Though Carlo Rossi would've sufficed,
broke out the '61 Chateau Calon Segur Saint Estephe,

its solid tannic backbone, cigar box nose (*Youthful
despite its age . . . I was really surprised it was still alive*).

HOLLY HOCK BAKERY'S MOVING TO MADISON VALLEY

So she's leaving us, dear Holly, for blacker forests,
for banana cream more creamy, for exponentially irresistible tarts.

So long, loganberry seven layer. Bon voyage, apricot chiffon.
Going, going, cinnamon buckle, gone.

Suddenly the birds at her feeder look good enough to eat.
She corners a white-throated sparrow, crunches his pretzel stick bones.

Like a child stuffing saltines into her mouth, whistling a tune, she
*Sam Peabody Peabody Peabody*s—grief escaping like feathery crumbs.

FALLING SHORT

There is a standard of perfection used in judging budgies. A perfect bird would receive a score of ten, but the perfect bird has yet to be shown and bred. –Know Your Budgie

You'd think that being mauve would be enough,
or opaline, cobalt, sky blue. You'd think
because your neck is ringed with spots
and you climb your latter faultlessly,

judges would flock to you, whisper *unmatched*.
What's wrong with them? Instead of noting
your robust breast as you mount your wheel,
instead of crooning to your rhymes,

they're pointing out your flat head, drooped tail,
faulty stance. What do they know, Budgie,
of your flawless leaps for chocolate cream pie?
Band too large, mask too small, lacks frontal rise

they scribble on their scorecards, neglecting to mention
you whistle songs. *Patchy color, nipped in neck, hangs over
perch* they criticize, failing to see a perfect bird
with their far from perfect eyes.

SELF-PORTRAIT IN THE STUDIO

with apologies to Salvador Dali

It doesn't matter what I wanted; now
I only want the fried egg on the plate

without the plate, the rose without thorns,
the child minus the whine. It is typical,

isn't it, this craving for what cannot be,
for the green by the fence that isn't ours?

It's so very expected to want honey,
not blood, to crave a marriage where

each head is a puffy cloud. If I could,
I would morph the ogre in the closet

into a soft monster who'd carry, instead
of a sword, a jiggly vat of vanilla pudding.

Sometimes all I desire is a piece of bread
expressing the sentiment of love. I don't need

to spurt like a fountain of milk spreading itself
uselessly on three shoes, to be the daddy

long legs of evening, to find the solution
to the puzzle of autumn; I don't hanker

to walk down the path to immortality (none
of it, none at all). What I long for is myself

with a healthy complexion, staring out
at a mystical sea, a Cathedral of thumbs

with which to play an invisible harp.

THE SAUSAGE PARADE

When the Roman Empire, like an overcooked
kielbasa, began to shrivel up, Christians made them

illegal. Peperone, Calabrese, Sanguinaccio:
from speakeasy kitchens, butter, lard, and onion

hissed. Holsteiner, Genoa, Cervelats:
Twenty centuries later, the High-Production

Pickle Injector ensures a steady supply.
Presskopf, Figatelli, Jagdwurst:

could it be their names? That each must form
to its casing? Whose nose hasn't longed

for the scent of fennel and pork?
Who can say *sausage* isn't onomatopoeic?

"Cook them slowly," *Dishes of the World*
insists. "To keep from bursting, prick."

Robert was my first: red pepper, pimento
pinch. Chorizo de Lomo. Taught me

sizzle, avoidance of smokehouse shrink. Never
would I settle for less. Byron Speer—oatmeal, vinegar

thyme—loved to go shirtless March to November.
Skin silken gravy, ovenbaked. Chuck, a Drisheen—

running ox, tansy-tinged; two parts blood
to one part cream. Helmut, all-hands-in-the-pot

simmering shallots, 6' 2", 220, sweetness
soaked (lawyer by day, Braunschweiger

by night); Dylan a Rotwurst, *keeping sausage—*
sage, chesnut purée, lemon, Muscadet—

would have kept and kept . . .

The man I love doesn't love my bread-crumb-soaked,
sputtering-pork-and-chipolata past—

salsicce, budini, zamponi.
But the past is long as Italy's boot.

It is made of leeks, red wine,
crushed garlic, whole peppercorns.

There is plenty of room at the table.

II. SUCH A WAY TO GO

WITH OUR SPIRITS HIGH AND OUR LIFEJACKETS PATCHED, WE CONSIDER A TRIP TO UNKNOWN WATERS

Our raft resembles a nest of mosquito eggs,
but we want to overcome our fear of rapids,
gather mussels, visit Hoover Dam.
We want to decide where it's safe to swim.

Weather permitting, we leave on Sunday morning.
We're not sure where we'll stop or stay
or which we prefer: oceans to rivers, crayfish to clams.
We're not sure which clothes we'll wear.

We've heard of deserted islands south of Florida.
We can't stop seeing neon tetras,
how they scattered when we tapped the glass.
We've read books on nudibranchs.

We are learning to be buoyant; we are learning
to hold our breath. We are bringing a pole, a pin,
some string. We are hoping for sturgeon, Maori Chiefs.
Perhaps we will float by the Temple of Dawn.

When we look in our shoes, there will be seaweed.
When we sleep we will dream of sand.
The water will be calm or swift. We will say to ourselves
what a wide, smooth highway this is.

BECAUSE I AM FULLY CONVERSANT WITH MY HIDEOUS QUALITIES

I'm forgiving of your channel catfish soul patch,
of your avian features—preen, strut, dive for the hedge,

for the trunk, for the loess; heck, you can always preen
in our makeshift master suite. Bring your elves!

They can help us dismantle the infrastructure,
its many robotic arms. Don't forget your lotus petals,

your ten easy tricks for ceasing desire. Because, yes,
I can write volumes in Old Church Slavic about my unsightly side,

recite my appalling faults like the Ten Commandants
x 99, including my not-so-righteous attempts at catch and release,

please bring along your five-pound bag of salt,
your towering pine, and we will drench our wounds,

and we will mangle that tree till it overtakes the yard
like a jaunty Venus de Milo; she will be the stranger within

the teetering fence. Thanks to her, we can sit by the hallowed
window where the spin of the earth whispers *latitude, travel, power.*

there were many *don'ts*: pirates, maidens, deer
resembling Bambi. And we were urged to be ourselves,
or selves, that is, who knew birds.
And if we had the nerve to begin
with a peer through a key hole
we knew what couldn't follow. Trees

had names, in other words—
Texas mulberry, one-seed juniper—
it was time to learn them. To steal
from cormorants, admire our shadows, sing.
To make sure, if our speaker drives a Kharman Ghia,
a semi destroys it. Pay attention

to your neighbor's yard. Juncos
plump in the rain. Beware of what you hate:
the reddest red neck loves. Listen
to chirping (rooms of industrious typists,
deep-pitched *jug-o-rums*, fingernails
running the teeth of combs). Observe

the slowly-opening tulip (once it reveals
its mysterious black, it's all over). Rip
the ring from your ear, the parrot
from your shoulder, unveil the innocent,
dismantle the fawn. Find the bird
that drums its wings like a car

that won't turn over, spend a year
with Richard Preston's *Trees*.
There is a toad, Henry, distant chorus
a diesel engine, engine you taught us
runs on compression. There is a bird,
ten years after the mill shut down,

still whirring like a circular saw.
On a warm night in early March, lost
in a maze of gray apartments, fooled
you're far from what sings, strain your ears.
This increases the odds. But I hear them,
Henry, and you're right: it isn't a *ribbit*,

any more than a creeper's a *seeseelookat me.*
You will fail most of the time. Mostly,
you will fail. You will find yourself
driving in circles, buildings marked
A, B, C. Always there will be singing you can't
put a name to—petals so perfect they fall.

IN PLACE OF A BLANK-FORM REJECTION SLIP

I wish I didn't have to dole them out like toxic poxes—
instructional how's, euphemistic no's. Truly, I'd rather

be minding my dozen heat-wracked hives, sanding down
the ledges of a rain-warped patio. As is my way, I don

my death mask, reach for my bag of *hope, try, admire,*
and as I'm reassuring, find myself falling into the deep

reverential abyss of a greasy spoon south of Roseburg,
the one where no one's ever denied, but given the choice

of bacon cheese, chicken, chicken fried. Oh, the ripple
and the toffee crunch, where one frigid lick unleashes

the far-off, faint flickering of the giant neon burger
in an ever-accepting sky. True, we only publish a few,

but know we value ketchup on a cheek or chin,
those moments between the ordering, the shouting

of a number all one's own. Little window with the door
shut tight against the heat, the cold, the, face it, next time

it'll be you I pleasantly scratch and sniff; a thanks not a *thanks,
but no thank*s, but no's opposite, wrong wrestled into right,

gusty gone gutsy, teetering away from a predominant
less than quite. Truly, I liked the shuffling slippers

and recalcitrant ants, especially how the waitress heaves,
instead of buckets of dehydrated onions, bolts of gabardine.

Meanwhile, your gray-tiled gatekeeper's napping while Vivaldi
blares, dozing like a feckless father, resurrecting the spectacles

of youth, drooling with keep us posted, not exactly lying
through crusty bicuspids as much as fibbing like the school girl

insisting she's off to punch the clock when clearly her heart's
being courted like a red patent leather shoe. Oh, shoot—

what I'm trying to say between sniffles and snores is not quite
I love you but something about the impressiveness of your ampersands,

your lemon-scented gerunds, that ever present toss between profundity
and mundane moroseness. We hope you do/don't feel as homeless

as that fellow who dwells in a cardboard box, which yesterday held
your neighbor's fridge. Please? I think you know it's easier to jaw

about the Cubs, breakers and squalls, the stubbly plains, than these kinda
enjoyed, these that didn't move us like a Navaho's *go*, word for which

they have 300,000 synonyms: *sayonara, won't be long, toot-a-loo*—language
more a portal than a place to rest, *nasha* ("something going from here

to there"), not the static road. The same way I'm running toward
every last one, sifting and sorting, all of them coming up short.

MY HOUR WITH JORIE GRAHAM

1.

I was supposed to buy her lunch.
All she wanted: the juice
of apples.

2.

Too ripe fruit
slit with a Henckels.
Moths surrounding
the runoff.

3.

Her mouth at a bottle shaped like an apple
(my mouth mute as an apple)

4.

My poem my pomegranate my brand new outfit
(The poem asking *whose poem is it?*
The poem unsure)

5.

Hadn't I read Keats
Hadn't I heard of the objective correlative

6.

Let the siskins and the artichokes speak for themselves!

98,000.2

God I hate this
(God in my mind of no mind God in the (swollen) sea & me without oars)

♉

Just-butterfly—the wet & vulnerable hour
Butterfly shirking the worm's pedestrian hunger . . .

🕐

all those layers
so many folds of gauzy black
I never did find where the fabric ended
(the fabric the thing concealing, the feeling untoward)
Draped like the partial torso of Iris
((((((of being wrong altogether, of her being altogether right))))))

💣💣💣

what it must've been for Helen . . .
(war of the seeking not to estrange, war of the coveted
apple)

🗁

We paused on the sidewalk
talked course loads, needy students, summers in Wyoming
I asked did she still find time to write
(in this ivy rancor in these halls washed free of sepulchral leisure)

(☺)

She smiled the smile of transcendence

13.

Goddess of tossed back hair & dirt-smudged pumps
Pulse's impulse
Some first-year's wettest dream
Damned if I'd consciously take your advice
Damn if I still don't find the finest powder
where I brushed against your wings

WHAT THE GRAD STUDENTS SAID

This is a terrific title, all your titles
should be this good—like a playground

with twirly and tunnel slides,
and a bathroom nearby to boot!

And all your poems should be as good
as this first one, which not only stood out

like a tilt-a-whirl on a flat bed broken down
along I-5, but reminded us of the words

we hate, like any compound adjective
and *scrunch*. We liked very much the one

with the Brain Gelatin Mold. Also the one
where Bly loses his luggage along with his smiling-

Buddha shtick at the Dodge. However, we didn't
get interested till *gingivitis* and, overall, we stopped

reading when we realized—by the third line—
you weren't even trying to reach us at all but instead

were yammering on to a nephew, son, sister, blah, blah, blah.
In other words, you weren't a finalist, runner-up, semi-finalist,

22nd or even 55th in line, but you were definitely
one of the 67 entrants! That, a little ketchup,

marmalade, vinegar, a few shakes of salt,
and a pinch of dried mustard will sure make a good

marinade for baby backs, but you thoroughly, definitely,
unredeemingly, did not in any way, shape,

or razzle-dazzle popsicle, come within
dozens of Mr. Natural paces from winning

our coveted prize.

JUST DON'T WRITE ANY POEMS ABOUT NIAGARA FALLS

—Richard Hugo

Nobody cares it's raining where you are.
Nobody wants to know a cumulonimbus
floats by your house like a sneezing frog. Keep it

to yourself. Keep too your mother's mother's
labored-over pansies—ivory petals bowing
like sheets on a pulley clothesline, morning

glories strangling your will as guilelessly
as the sky. We've already read the one about
the hamster in the foxglove, so we won't

be alarmed when it turns out to be
a baby possum, nor will we stick around
for your *splendid marsupial triumphant evolution*

song. Nobody cares, in other words,
about your childhood: gargantuan zucchinis,
ailing mimosas, the day your father sliced

your beach ball with his pocket knife when it crushed
a struggling tomato; Snooper and Peeka, Ashes and Butch;
your various hunches as to the origins of a large, rectangular-

with-round-depression rock, perfect birdbath for grackles
and starlings: Lenape bed pan, meteor, Yapese dime.
If we have to read one more time about your return

to Grove Ave. in the spring of '95, finding your bubble gum pink
and ever-lintful hyacinth choking beneath the vent for the dryer,
or imagine your breaking voice as you grope to describe

the stranger among your Uncle Peter's wrapped-in-the-*Kansas-City
Star*-and-carried-from-Tightwad-Missouri comfrey (comfrey
which proceeded to blanket the entire yard), if you then not

so surreptitiously segue into tales of two-foot snows
cushioning your *N*s (*Needs Improvement*, you got them in
"Follows Directions"); stroke, in other words, that tiniest violin

of a weatherful, kittenful, puppyful, *o great vanished youth*,
grandmother-inspired yarn, and we're cursing you:
in your next life you'll be the maintenance guy

at Niagara Falls in ticking coveralls, name embroidered
above your heart—the one in charge of the Giant Valve,
releasing pressure for newlyweds and tourists, ensuring

water flows at a rate they can gush at. When they've finished
(*what a beautiful day the day we met . . . I'm so glad your grandma
let slip her passion for miniature poodles . . . Snuggles would love*

this place! Did I ever tell you I came here as a child . . .), when
they want to know if it's worth springing for a valentine tub
or a boat ride to the Cave of the Winds and the trilobite wall,

you'll be the one they turn to for advice.

MY QUESTION ISN'T WHY DID THEY HIT US

but why didn't they hit us more?
Because the boy in the ad ran

through sepia streets longing for home,
on Tuesday we slurped *Prince* spaghetti.

Because Robin Gerber owned a Suzy
Homemaker Oven *and* Bouncy Baby.

Who can explain, to a child, capitalism?
Doesn't it make more sense to grab

a stick *don't you ever* (swat) *ever* (swat)
ever? Sneaking into their secret drawers,

eating their favorite Brach's (caramels
with frosting hearts), peering through

their bedroom door keyhole to their stock-still
nakedness (Did they sense us? Freeze? Reason,

like beetles, lack of motion would save them?)
Stealing with our giggles *I'm telling* teasing

whining any hope for a finishing thought.
Father attempting to study stifling our peals

blowing guffaws out our noses oh we tried
but not enough. Milk and meatball laughter
spraying the dining room rug.

WHAT I MEANT TO SAY BEFORE I SAID "SO LONG"

for Dante Alfredo Silano

There will be spiders the size of your ears, drinks
that will make you stupid, matches you'll long
to strike; there will be mop-ups the size of Rhode Island.

Or you'll be driving at night beneath the cloud-hidden
Perseids, but the car in front will lose a wheel, spray
a million sparks. The spider won't drop its strand

above your bed but choose a far corner. Don't kill it:
what it spins will rival what hangs from your neighbor's
hedge. Your father loves what shines—the flash

in the pan, two-penny nugget glint, what might lead him
from buckets, latex, brush's swish, loves the gleam
that was you in his eye. As a child he built fires

beneath a rising Dog Star, ignored the heat,
his mother's no's, heard only *go ahead, Matty-boy,*
my tee-too, my shaver, build whatever you like.

Loved what was left when the brightness died,
to fish the yard for the stubs of rockets. What he kindled
in Ash Flat—eight miles from Evening Shade, lift of Earth

that is Ozarks—he feeds logs to now (last stop being the flashing
CHAINS REQUIRED), where the spark between him
and your mother . . . where you were born. Ashland.

Which must be why they named you Dante, an unlit match
held close to a blaze. He pans for gold, tells us by the crow's
fly (by the eagle, by the osprey) we're close to a mine, scars

in the side of a hill, close to where the flood of '64 tore the earth,
unearthed the glimmers he dreams of. He's got scars on his back,
stretches of road he can't recall but don't be scared: all that fire-

water's behind him, the bottomless tap, beer after golden beer.
His love for explosives cost him all the gold in the Applegate Valley,
"Possession of a firearm" emblazoned on screens from Metuchen

to Tucson—*a pellet gun; I shot at the sky.* Not that we're here
forever, not that we don't live in the shadow of live volcanoes,
the chance we'll wake to at least a dusting of ash. *So long,*

trooper, I managed to say, your father asking for Roman Candles,
Dancing Bees, Flower Clusters, *stuff that shoots out sparks.*
South of Eugene, two-hundred miles from your eager hands,

the sun through clouds a million motionless searchlights,
I began to fall in a trap: *Don't let boredom grip you*
the way you gripped my finger; let even the seemingly

starkest places yield you black-eyed Susans; learn from the woman
who with her entire body tells you "I've done all this."
Since each of us will soon be part of the meal,

since we're more like tents than mountains, and mountains
disappear . . . (spinning, sinking, fuel light an ember,
finally sputtering out).

AT THE SHOREBIRD FESTIVAL: GRAYS HARBOR COUNTY, WA

We're learning their names: dunlin, black-bellied plover.
Sandpipers: western and least. Styles of probing:
run, stop, run; incessant sewing machine. What's
diagnostic: upturned bill of the slender, elegant
avocet. Ruddy turnstone's crimson feet.

Wired for wind and cold, bills conveniently tuck
beneath scapulars; feet retreat to feathered bellies.
At the slightest hint of shadow, sudden movement
(ring-billed gull, drifting leaf), they take to the air
like giant, swirling amoebas, locust dark till they turn

in a flash of white—beautiful, undulant whirl
lowering the odds of a raptor's successful strike;
mournful *tu tu tu* of dowitcher, raucous *cur-ret* of the knot
translating unmistakably: *watch out*. Every movement,
ounce, sound, rigged for survival. But we're not thinking

life or death, the why of insulation, skittishness. We're focused,
as always, on something else: *American coot, osprey near bridge*
to Aberdeen (mill stench, strip mall, though equaling loss, unworthy
of note), a nearby curmudgeon's grumble ("the brochure said
thousands . . . "), what's for lunch—mortality's access,

like the nesting grounds of snowy plovers,
all but permanently blocked. Even when we turn
from mudflat to ocean, to the surfer stuck in a crisscross
of breakers refusing to spit him out—bobbing, waving his arms—
to four Jeep Cherokees emblazoned *Ocean Shores Police*

barreling down the beach, to a man—wild-eyed, mustachioed—
heading out in a boat to save him, routine, we're thinking.
And as he guns the motor, greets each surge—head high,
bulging chest—as he enters the whirling churn,
we're unconcerned enough to admire

the sunlight pouring down in silvery rays,
magnificent concert of every-which-way waves.
Even when two massive swells converge to flip his boat,
and *he's* the one who's waving *I'm okay.* Rising. Falling.
Disappearing. Surf a vortex . . . rushes . . . rips . . .

And just as we're getting nervous (police, walkie-talkies, a growing,
gawking crowd), *was he wearing a wetsuit isn't ten minutes all it takes?*
out of nowhere a Coast Guard lifeboat nabs the surfer,
while a faint, growing louder, whir-and-heart-pounding-
clomp-clomp-clomp of a chopper lowers in

on the place where . . . *but now I don't see him is he*
he's under blinding swirl of water and blades,
a man on a rope plunging into *he can't be did you see*
his eyes did you see the squall, comes up with a body,
a body, limp as a . . . limp as a . . .

he's okay, the wind knocked out that's all hoists him up
like a half-mast flag on a windless day *he sure looks*
dead like a dead man have you ever seen someone living
hang like that like the suit's empty to shore where medics
he'll be okay those who knew him cradling their own

incredulous faces, a round of *shits* pacing static *no*
response no one asking *is he?* Huddled. Stunned.
Light draining the sky. The last *good God. Good-*
night. Even after the tide erases every footprint,
and where he lay a flock of whimbrels alights.

A TRIP THROUGH THE YELLOW PAGES: BA, BE, AND SO FORTH

We begin with Babbitting, Beckwith & Kuffel, then quickly
move on to Babies: Top Stoppers, breast pumps, Lifetime

Furniture. There's Stork Express, Go to Your Room,
merry-go-rounds and Pre-Learning Inc.,

but before we get the scoop on in-the-womb
teaching, we're onto black flow, Badge Express,

Button King. What next? Burlap.
Who are we calling? Lacey O'Malley, Bail Bondsman.

Where to? Both Ways Catering. *Everything She Touches
Tastes Terrific*, the ad for LUV-N-OVN says, *Just Dial EAT-*

CAKE, and we will, but we must move on to Balemaster, True Wheel,
Large Capacity Portable Stands, must pick a barrel to hold

our waste, choose from the largest selection of towel bars
in the West. Then onto Aurora for retail, wholesale, Life

Plus, then smack in the middle of bushings, bearings,
cowplugs—which brings us to Beauty (sheaves

to shears)—Adam & Eve, A Cut Above, Connie
and her Class Act. Now that we're weaved and braided,

coiffed and permed, trimmed and waxed, now that acrylic
adorns our nails (two weeks guaranteed), we find ourselves

in Adjustable Beds, Quality Down for Fifty Years, Comforter
Kits. Let us Sit-N-Sleep, then let us be lifted from our remote

control rest (factory direct), past idlers, pulleys, and PVC
to the heaven of Prompt Response and champagne fountains.

SUCH A WAY TO GO

But that's how it is. One minute battling traffic. Next, head
in an oven, inner kingdom hospital blue—cool and soothing

glacier, what a baby boy comes home in. With a sparkling
silver toothbrush, the blanket's unsinged. De-ashed. Daisy

Marble, Butter Sponge removed. And what satisfaction!
Such blue brilliance—spent comets, star cinders—loosened

with Ajax. With force. No wonder she chose this: rising
crescents, soft braids, perfect white. Left her children

(bread and milk). The pan too large. Under. Over. Not
quite done. Tick and bang of a cold place heating.

Head where flour, water, salt. Peaks before they fell.

ODE TO OLFACTORY

Prometheus moth: how closely we resemble thee,
your limbic-system-driven chase, how far we roam

to get it on in a forest of twisted Egyptian sheets, to inhale
a loved one's weedy breath. How far we hike to be enveloped

in a minty, mind-stopping, bergamot-loud cloud, reveling
in its nose-tickling resemblance to basil, lavender, rosemary.

Opposite of what my father slammed into when he opened the door
of his sister's Miami apartment three weeks after she killed herself,

not her father's budding black-red roses, a Pine Barrens lake.
More like a quail defrosting on a dissecting table. O Proust

and your madeleine, I believe what you say about nibbling
a lemony sponge, how a few small crumbs replaced life's dread

with *precious essence*, but how much swifter the trigger
from attic trunk mothballs to summer's pungent start,

from Dr. Rankin's pain-disguising clove oil to the memory
of his hairy hand in my mouth. O so quicker than what childhood

served up—crumble, kuchen, kugel, velvet soup. In the Yakima Canyon
we rub sagebrush between thumb and forefinger, recall

with a shake of the head the error in thinking it cooking sage.
Rotten-egg stench of overworked catalytic converters,

sunny-side uppers sizzling and popping, aroma of plastic fruit
from a long-lost board game: Hi Ho Cherry O. Fallen fir

as its resins release, sun dried seaweed. Return us to the ocean's
incessant babble of deadness. Sawdust: whatever you said.

PAGE TURNERS

Rodeo star meets Nazi-resister,
battles deadly assassin; 30-somethings
sit shiva. Father performs highwire act
between towers, encounters werewolf.
Tracking celebrity chef, Freedom
Fighter trades in AK-47
for potato peeler. Many shades
of love: finger-lickin', psychic, long-
lost, vampiric. Plenty of Fool's Gold,
political turmoil. Racecar driver/
Supermodel recalls impoverished
youth as dying clock repairman.
Conjoined twins reunite in the Urals.
Thanks to little bee/lab-terrier mix,
darkest lie morphs to lilting song
for the lucky alchemist declaring
Game over! Epilepsy, demons reign.
Countless defectors, countless
estrangements, struggles in Maine
and Sonoma. But brazen brides
find key to invisible force field, render
haunting a rumor, while elephant rescues
tilt-a-whirl, girl who plays with fire…
and this is where they leave you.

SHRIMP ARITHMETIC

From the Restitution Desk, from the almost inhabitable pools
of piping heat, from ergonomically designed and tapering

treatments (13 by 7, 9 by 6), from toothpick tests
and *take deep breaths*, his adversarial posture nearly

escapes you. Here, take the numerator, the years
he contributed wages. Take what you can—

golf clubs, mail, egg shells. The megaphone pleading
meet your party—meet your party at the driving range.

While the crumpled leaf in the telephone wire
is a bird, its two legs holding,

the outstretched cormorant's only completely
himself. Did you dream of parrots,

then see one perched on a stranger's shoulder,
green as the swirl on a stagnant lake? Search

for a sign—*Alterations*—squint the crucial *c*?
The National Vessel Documentation Center

harbors in Falling Waters, and the judge awards
a portion—black bottom, marble, seven-layer.

As if you wanted cake.

RESPONSE TO A LETTER FROM MY EX

So I'm a statue now, Bernini-smooth,
stuck in a room on Villa Borghese, larger
than life, without a hint of scent or hair, perfect
in your memory? Damn you and your skill
with stone, your willingness to make my absence
beautiful. When we were in that park two years ago
your indifference nearly ruined me. Remember
how you read your *Herald*, waved away
who Daphne was? You hated statues, churches,
art—whatever wasn't news from home, a way
to make me look incompetent. Now I read
you loved me all along, though then you wouldn't
take my picture, refused to let me buy a piece of lace.

Marble's cold against your skin, keeps you full
of compliments. Listen: I never was anything but feeling-
covered bone—messy, unchiseled, mutable. Riotously
human, I am not what you chose to turn away from
those awful days in Rome.

THEY'RE PROHIBITED BY CITY ORDINANCE

but if I were a horse, I'd eat like one.
Face against the wind, win you over

with my longing for apples. I'd be skittish,
with my own particular fears. Saddle-

flinching. Cantering, but only when you want me
to trot. If I were a horse, I'd be proud

of all sixteen of my hands. Which hay,
which paths, when to be put out to pasture:

I'd know. You'd be braiding red yarn into my tail,
warning others I kick, blaming my meanness

on the apples. And I'd kick you. I'd kick you.

IN NATURE ONE SELDOM SEES CIRCLES

Unless, of course, one happens to have a nose,
or a mole, or a pair of nipples (stamens and stigma
enflaming a wild rose); unless one closes in
on pores, imagines an egg gliding down a tube
while moving oneself toward a moon, its lovely,
convolutional whole. Unless one's never noticed
pebbles, what a pebble thrown in a pool can do.
No bellies, contemplated seasons, orifical glows.
Unless, on a sunny day, surprisingly, ones looks up.

A STALK OF WINTERBERRIES

They were giggling rouge.
They wore cherubic lipstick.

Fiery. Festively, diminutive.
Clustered and drunk. Rutilously

guffawing. Scarlet corralled
since college. One of them

wears a vermillion slip.
One of them hails

from a burnished wood; one
a sanguine celebrity sporting

a ruby-red Triumph. Much mirth,
much ruddy sighing. Degrees

in feverish, in wiping the sweat
from a mother's blazing forehead.

Much Bordeaux. Many combustible
memories—variegated, stalked. Cheery

with a touch of flaming. Many-faceted
mini-cardinals. Twig as a ray of cancer.

The daughter of one approaching
the bloody edge of moon, the sister

of another dabbling like a roseate
spoonbill. Not one of them infallible.

All of them seeing red.

THE ROUTE BLOOD TAKES TO THE HEART

Have you heard them at night
over your house your yard
huh-HONK huh-HONK
a little mournful a little joyous
why you love the moss jading
the cracks of roofs under the moon
the pear tree holding a few dead leaves
till a warm week in incongruous March
the whitest blossoms blanket your porch
and you're cornered, must consider living
and dying overlap In the wind their feathers
move like moths the color of aging mushroom gills
prehistoric-kneed they wobble toward you
their willingness to risk   I want to touch one *there*
you say   pointing where droplets stick to feathers
tightly packed   of the pair en route to Magellan Island
on foot because a broken wing   injured coaxed by the strong
the grass like cows they seemed content with until they eyed
your loaf Crumbs cover their bills the bag's empty
still they ask with tongue and neck for more

IN THAT OTHER UNIVERSE

I married you—all your useless
gadgets, all your mother's wishes
I were Jewish, all my almost perfect
birthday pound cakes, all your kindness,
all your kindness (all my doubts).

Our best man brought the abalone
rings, snow peas, *rughetta*, chanterelles.
My best friend caught the broccoli flowerets.

After the stroll through spaghetti,
hubbard, and delicata, after the artichoke
toss and pin the turnip on the navel,
after the toasts and the long good-bye,
we honeymooned on an island
ninety miles along where long-

necked stilts predicted falsely our demise.
Days we'd shop for chervil, capsicum, basil.
Nights we'd point to constellations—cilantro,
asparagus, savory. We thought of having everyone

for dinner, then listened to the tui. We thought
of having everyone: the sleeping sea gull, head
tucked under a wing, the bones of emus.

We thought of sending invitations: come as you are,
tomato. And rock wren, riflebird, gannet: RSVP.
And the waves began to whisper *Good choice,*
Good choice, Good choice, in that other universe,
on a planet like a patty-pan squash.

II. WHAT THE TRUTH TASTES LIKE

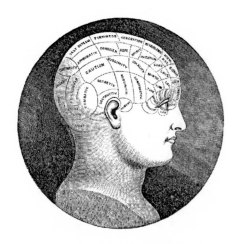

WHAT'S FREE

broken cement

tubing

fill dirt

wire

the rusty cast-iron skillet my ex-roommate
left me before she lit out for Toad Suck, Arkansas
(it wouldn't season)

Saul's Swingline stapler
jamming and skipping

cracked aquarium
with gratis eau de turtle

The Art of Technical Writing

Real Skills

*

nothing's free
my father used to say
but he was wrong:

pine cones and sticks
that magically transform
into fairy houses

a favorite pair of holey hand-me-down sweats

walking into Canada
by way of Horseshoe Basin

FULL TILT

Hopefully you're not pinned between a cable
and a crashing gondola, hopefully not on the clock

but busy catching bulldog stargazers, reckoning the cloud
above you resembles not a sheep but a giant wad of Orbit.

Here it's a Saturday at the Full Tilt Arcade & Creamery,
cases freshly loaded with Mango Chili, Golden Guernsey Honey,

Vegan Coconut Chunk, quarters jangling in my pocket, poised
to be shoved into the slot for a round or four of The Simpsons

Pinball Party, and just as the first ball pops on deck, in walks a woman
asking for vacuum cleaner bags. *Everything's digitized!* I yell between slurps

of Roxbury Road, between gentle bumps with alternating hips
to increase my chances of getting the ball to land smack-dab

on Homer's light-up nose. *Why don't you program your vacuum
to empty itself?* But this only confounds her more, this gal who

just snuck up through a crack in the pavement direct from the Menlo Park
Woolworth's, its doors shuttered since 1979. Maybe Target, I offer.

You would think, she scowls, making her way toward
the treacherous, creamless, pingless street. *You would think.*

DO NOT TOUCH THE ART

Don't sip the structure.
Don't suck the slab.
With the wind do not embrace.

Do not kinetically sway.
Brushstroke by brushstroke, do not broaden.
Do not partake.

Don't grope the Gorky.
Don't bear upon the blurring.
Don't diminish with your contribution.

Don't woo the welded.
Don't probe the pastiche of longing and loss.
Butt off the furniture, buddy.

Do not tap the totemic.
Do not lick the verbal.
Do not fall in love.

Don't ucky the upward.
Don't fog the relief.
Do not scuff the drama.

Don't thumb the untransformed.
Don't denude the negation.
Get your oils away from these oils.

Don't paw, outsider!
Suppress your arouse.
Stick your increase in a bucket with the snuffed out cigs.

TO THE WOMAN WHO, WHEN I WENT TO HEAT MY PIZZA
   IN THE OFFICE MICROWAVE, ASKED ME, "WHO ARE *YOU?*"

I am ranked the Highest Order, Most Benevolent
Devilled Eggs, i.e., Most Honored Toothless Machu Picchu,
gracious Queen of Ouzel Dust. I was voted Most Likely
to Hug a Flammable Ranch and Miss Grow a Sputnik
on Your Face. In church I drink the spots
from Lucy Spigman's dress. In Bartell Drugs I pray
to muscle rub. Before you now I place an artist's sketch,
fully rendered, fully built of horsehair lamps
and an orange couch (40% broasted, 40% rapeseed,

30% duff). I invented the perpetually grieving
Linzer-torte and the self-effervescing catbox lid.
I am first in Oil of Amphibian samovars, Silly Putty
tabletops, and sipping sprigs. I've yet to lose
a carob-coated raisin race, and I finished 45th at 23rd
and 61st at 3.2.8. I know, in short, of ants who'll eat
an earwig's leg for lunch. Regrettably, I've never
owned a boat, but I've seen Helen Farkus flinch.
Rest assured: documents I carry prove my worthiness.

FOR A FRIEND WHO SENDS ME A FLYER ON THE ART OF EAR CANDLING
AND NEWS HER BOOK HAS ARRIVED

Could it be true? That a hollow taper,
poised at the edge of an ear, ignited,
sucks out year of "interesting contents"?
Drawn by a narcissistic yearning to see
your own wax, would you risk a loss
of hearing? Swabs, it says, are detrimental,
cannot reach the depths. "Upon inspection,"

would the flame extrude, in the form of mites,
your mother the harbinger's *honey, the belt
goes around your waist . . . blue side down*?
Does your father's *yastupiddummydon't
gimmeanyofyourguff* swell like fungus
the size of a brain coral? What about
his *don't be talking*, which lodged itself
in a clump so thick (in the oval window?
in the bony labyrinth?) it echoes your
every word? What if it *did* loosen (gently,

with crackling, with hissing) every fluid
movement, every cumulonimbus-shaped
incus vibration, every ounce of sound
within thirty-three years of earshot?
Could you have it pick and choose?
Could you rig it, for instance, so it only
softens the good stuff, the *You, Yes, YOU*s?
Could you have it skip the refusals, the *let's
just be friends*, Mr. Hoppel's lawn mower
drowning out the robins at dusk, Bobby
Whitman's Chevy the 99th time before
it turned over? What is wax but food for flame?

And you're waxing, Debi. This is the time
to pick corn, Whitman's *full-noon trill*,
the time to let loosen amber kernels
of grief, your time to shine.
Rolled in your ears the ancient waxing—
Goddess Diana—rolled in your ears

what's kept our friendship incandescent
(two cradled receivers, two lobed doubloons).

And *Oyyyyyy!* your letter cries (every bird
that sang singing again). You heard stomping,
a loud knock, then leapt for the door; your voice
gleaming over seven machines before it hits you:
this is mine, this my own. Book you know like the lines
ringing your mouth, lines of sound, vibrating bone.
How small the part we see (squiggles and curlicues
sway where a Q-tip never dreamed). One tube's
named for Bartolommeo Eustachio; there's a vestibule,
a stirrup, a drum (the mind flickers with all it cannot
know); the tragus barely tells the prologue . . .

I'm tempted, Debi—tempted to *feel a lightness
in the head*, to use it as an ancient stenographer:
*to write upon wax laid on boxwood, to form,
with an iron stylus:*

OF COURSE YOUR EARS ARE BURNING!

But what if this candling did do damage?
Turned *rapport* to *purulence*?
Made what we've pigeon-holed disappear,
left us with only the *hroo-hroo* of doves?

Notice how this Chris Coppens Coons, Certified
Candler, makes no reference to sticking or spearing,
to lancing or drilling, to dirking, plunging, forcing
or spiking, mentions only *receiving* massage,
involving the use of a candle.

Nope, we can't risk it. Can't give up
how we hear a song first (mother, father,
yellow-rumped warbler), then rout out
the body. Nor the chance to strain our ears
for the heart of a baby long before he swims
the canal. Can't risk losing the riff and jam
of our whole-balla-wax, can't-hold-a-candle-to
jags. Like two Black Turbans we cling
to what's shaped us—held by the roar of the sea.

MEN OF THE STONE AGE HAD NO USE FOR FRACTIONS

Neither do I. Who wants a piece
of cracker, chocolate cookie bite?
Who wants what's left at the bottom of the bag?
Give me the whole hog.
Give me salt pork, fat back, jowls.
Give me knuckles and cracklings, headcheese and lard.
Let me lick the grease from my fingers,
then lie on a couch, sated, lambent-lipped, no room to squeeze
a quarter ounce.

Spare me the snippets, shavings, scraps.
Spare me nips and drams.
Not the clause but the sentence.
Not the sentence but the tome.
(No piece without its pieces; no part without its whole.)

Give me the fish with the head intact.
Let me stare at the eye—never-melting hailstone, tapioca pearl.
Give me the eggs and their shells—blood spot, albumin.
Give me the skillet carried by covered wagon, Maverick, U-Haul.
Baltimore nonstick. Whippany Teflon.

Whatever a shebang is, I want it.
And leave in the pits, the seeds, the core.
Bring me everything and don't peel it.
(The crumbs I'll feed to the crows.)

SCHADENFREUDE

When the trampoline showed up unannounced,
I got giddy when your big toe kept finding

the stitching's gaps. When you lose the James Beard Award,
10,000 teaspoons short of the Clafouti Galaxy, it isn't a reach

to guffaw. Paprika, in fact, has always been a favorite,
especially when it's simmering in a soup of tarnished

trophies. I'm happy when Jupiter's storms sputter out,
when the cowboy loses his bowlegged gait, trades in

chaps for khakis. I hope your gumption's out of gas,
broken down on the side of Sad Sack Road; I hope

your razzle dazzle's fizzled, your best broomstick
frayed, dejuiced. When your last ex settles down

in Texas, that's my cue to grin. When your ball lands
in a trap, I snatch up the shiny tee, work it like a toothpick.

Inscribed on my gravestone: loved every minute of watching
your win-win go double loss, your happy horseshoe morphing

to a hex.

WHAT THE TRUTH TASTES LIKE

Though Homer used them to capture
a restless Odysseus ("like a man roasting

cotechini, eager to eat"), though their spice
and shape, link to orgy forced Constantine

to ban them, though Kafka, sick with fear
and sleeplessness, wrote of the urge

to lick one, it wasn't all a sausage parade—
Bratwurst, kielbasa, kishka. *Saucisses au Muscadet.*

Some of us hail from the realm of bread—
most open of open sandwiches. And if

we've been wooed by chorizo-full wisdom
(*Philosophers are like breasts . . .*), precoital

M80s, boasted *clove-studded onion, raw
egg, half his weight lean bacon,* likened

toes to mini-mortadelle, temperament
to cream lowered into boiling water

gently, if we sliced and sliced again
through the darkest crusts, shaped

that inner softness into love; if we're far
from what's juniper-berried, rubbed

with mint and marjoram—smoke
and casings, duel with the cholera-soaked

Plockwurst, of the moon and pen—
we were always more than a pillow,

pretty and plump, more than a bun
where a frank might lay its head.
Bangers, Boudoin Blanc, Copocolla—

like mankind's rockets they burst;
the juice runs down our backs.

TOO SMALL FOR INTELLECT, BIG ENOUGH FOR LOVE

early 20th* century obstetrics text describing a woman's brain*

My grandmother wasn't a chemist, but in her kitchen I learned
precision, science of dollop, pinch. She didn't own

a thermometer, measured heat with a dab to her wrist.
Yeast foamed like the incoming tide at Love Ladies Beach,

like drops of HCl in a test tube filled with zinc. Kneaded
not by machine so that now I can't enter my kitchen, touch

bowl, sugar, flour, wooden spoon without her long-earned
confidence dissolving the shame of a hundred chem lab flops:

scales so sure weight changed with a breeze, easily smashed
pipets, terror of Bunsen burner, meniscus more a reason

to pause (water smiling!). Without her hands on mine:
Feel how that feels? Now you're ready for rising.

TOWARD AN UNDERSTANDING OF MY SO-CALLED CALLING

It's my mother's fault.
When I squirmed in church,
craned to count, on the bridges

of stern parishioners, horn-rims
and cat eyes; when I looked up,
not in search of light or truth,

but to fill the wooden beams
with loopy, imagined script;
when her glance, which I'm sure

could stop me now, failed to halt
my swinging legs, she'd grab her purse
(an eye on me, an eye on the priest),

dig past needles, rows of knit and purl,
lipstick bright as flamingos, ubiquitous
tissues, the silvery rain hat folded down

to one thick, snapped-down strip, hand me
paper and pen. Blame my father, post-cookout
stargazer, astronomically enthusiastic (*lots*

of kids have burgers; how many Seven Sisters?),
who taught the comfort of wandering
Cassiopeia. The ones that moved, he said,

were ours. Blame them both, their painstaking
passions—infinitesimal, all-consuming,
pointless as too-far-off-to-warm-us stars,

as a great, great grandmother's tightly woven
bun, which though I never saw it unfurl,
was rumored to fall to her knees.

THE 1238 CHERRY AVENUE CREDO

I believe in waking early—effortless drift from dream to dawn
like a browned-in-the-oven loaf. First light on a pink brick wall.
There's nothing wrong with hand-me-downs, fog, getting lost
in a flame. I'm not convinced, in the event of a water landing,
seat cushions will save us, or that childhood hamsters ever die.
I vote no for ostrich rides, bowling where the scoring's computerized.
You gotta earn your bread and butter, my Polish grandmother says.
Make mine crusty Italian, rosemary-riddled, extra-virgin dipped.

LETTER FROM HERE

Whatever happened to Jamie Feltovic, Judy Schoenburger,
Taryn Wenk? Where's Jamie right this second, who ran beside me

in the hundred yard dash? Where's Judy, her favorite album of 1977
Fleetwood Mac? Where o where are Taryn's white patent leather

go-go boots? My mind swirls like this cottonwood fluff floating
through rush hour, over Long's Drugs, scurrying across streets

till it lands right here on Lake Washington, covers it with fluffy dots.
Mother Nature had a plan: overdo it, just in case—which is why

I'm here and you're here, and Jamie and Judy and Taryn,
if they're alive, if they haven't succumbed to a growth,

an unreasonable girth, if they didn't take the low road
toward gout. A lot of time since I last saw them, or Tommy Lux

or Gary Gazda. A lot of time, a lot of drawbridges up and down,
ankles turned and imploded domes, many gallons of milk whisked

along highways in shiny cylindered tanks, on, for instance,
this floating span ending with signs whose directions

I can't quite make out. What became of the D'Alfonsi twins?
Was it I who was smitten with Richard, my best friend swooning

for Bruce? Or was it the other way around? (Only Joanie Hoppel
can tell me—but who knows over which hotel she presides?).

If I could call you, Bobby Westowski, I'd remind you of the swirled
stack of brown clay we placed on a sidewalk, waited for a classmate

to step. If I could reach you, Donna Marty, first I'd ask, of course,
all about you, but then right in about a town pirouetting with chum

and silvers, with ants struggling up twigs, bumble bees
clinging to the infamous lavender. About the geese, how they're gentle

till you get between two adults and their young. What's your profession,
Wendy Hoover? What did you make of yourself? My making

is yet to be surmised. Let's call me Great Lover of Cottonwood Fluff,
Impeccable Revere-er of Fecundity, Devotee of All Things Lapping, Lunging.

AT THE HOOT 'N HOLLER GUEST HOUSE IN UNCERTAIN, TEXAS

I yank off my tennies, take a load off, take a long, gawky gaze
at Gamma Cygni, patchy pink and purple milky swirl

the Arabs named *Hen's Breast*, worthy nod to the tastiest
part of the bird, especially when deep fried, lifted

from a grease-dotted paper bag to suck the meat
from the rubbery cartilage. And heck, forgot the napkins.

I'm licking my fingers one by one, totally apropos
here in these Piney Woods, with the ghoulish

Spanish Moss, with the bobwhite belting out its name.
I will sleep late, then linger in my Freedom

Kitchen not overlooking the lake. After I've lost
four games of solitaire, I will charcoal grill and smoker;

I will electric hookup because the boathouse and den
truly are a hoot 'n holler, as are the ceiling fan

and patchwork bedspread; I am going to rock
my cypress knees into a screen porch revelation,

way past the swamp buggies and the trotlines,
toward Sadachbia, *Lucky Star of Hidden Things*.

I DREAM A KIND OF PEACE,

you know the kind, bellbird or blue jay, whippoorwill
or white-headed babbler. Uneventful. No one having woken

to a burglar crawling through a kitchen window in search
of a big screen TV, not one jerboa or neighbor, coyote trickster

or Egyptian jackal demanding your bowl of gruel, your hand,
your life. *Comme si, comme ça. Ça va bien.* The sky, as for eons,

growing paler, the usual headlines as you switch off the front porch light:
One-armed man applauds the kindness of strangers. Dream a kind of peace

where planarians slink toward dawn, beating cilia to their pond scum song.
Calm enough for that one-armed man to begin the dream of regeneration,

dream in which we all become entangled in Quantum Entanglement,
forgetting whose God's chasing what tail. A kind of peace where a mother

might call not to tell you the fighting has resumed, but to help you pronounce
Julius Caesar. YOO-lee-us KYE-sahr, YOO-lee-us SAY-sahr,

electrons, protons, molecules stomping a country-swing hootenanny,
a honky-tonk immeasurability, what Einstein referred to as *spooky action*

at a distance, where a thing like peace might gain momentum, spin.

SHOES LIKE SNOW

He thinks he might have met her in a bank.
She's the kind who prattles (*I met this guy . . .*),

leaves her wooden window, hides in the safe
counting dimes. The other tellers hate her.

When he, his check and deposit slip arrive
$68.85, she says out loud: *$68.85.*

Or she's the kind who slides what he'd never buy
on his feet warm from high-tops: wing-tipped Florsheims.

How do they feel, she asks. He walks around, stops
in every mirror, slanted, knee-high. Rubs his neck,

preoccupied. Wants to see her shoehorn, ease her into every shoe
in stock, help her find the mates to all the ones abandoned

on Route 9. And she follows. They stand in traffic, ask each driver
idling at the light: *Where are the shoes? When are they coming back?*

The drivers think they want to wash their windshields,
attempt to buy them away with dollar bills. What does it mean

to wait for the other shoe to drop they ask the housewife, lawyer,
the guy driving Hugh's Appliance Truck. It starts snowing

shoes, tongues they haven't seen since childhood. He thinks
they might have met in Torrance, he might have known

the sewer grate she and Crystal Asmar sat atop on humid
afternoons, he might have been among the ones she chased,

she might have found him spinning like the teacher asked,
in Thrifty where the food was cheap, in the Pacific.

And the weather bears them leather uppers, spiked heels,
rubber soles, heavy accumulations, not one pair unmatched.

JOY

If Joy gets in your eyes, rinse thoroughly with water.
If swallowed, drink a glass of water to dilute.

For months, O Proctor & Gamble, I have had joy in my eyes,
though I have been rinsing with water. Joy isn't something
I'd want to rinse from my eyes, even if it were possible,
even if a loss of Joy would smooth away my laugh lines.
O Joy, your strength does more than clean handwashables.

One night, I opened my mouth and swallowed Joy
by the gallon. Who on this spinning earth
would choose to dilute such jubilance?
I am planning a trip to your home in Cincinnati, Ohio,
and I will be bringing my party horns.

O Patent Number 4,133,779,
may I always avoid the fumes that arrive
from mixing you with Clorox. Enraptured, all smiles,
may I never waste my bliss scrubbing dirty bottles.
May Joy remain forever in my eyes.

SPELLCHECK CHANGES *SILANO* TO *SALINE*

but I don't mind—ever-tearful,
ever-nicknamed Pickles Queen.
Lover of brine—splash zone,
pelagic, sub-littoral. Home
where the ocean's near. Ever
drawn to the true point
of beginning—horse shoe crabs
on a Wildwood beach, crinoid lilies
swaying shallowly. What, after all,
is *Silano*? Father's father's father's . . .
eighteen *greats* to Senator Eppio,
richest of Roman blood, but just
one quarter, while under a tugging sea—
Katrosh, Bullock, Pickarski. *Mother's
maiden name, please* (underside
of who we are, shadow self, whispering).
With a name like Saline maybe I'd befriend
the crepuscular thick knees, glimpse
magellanic plover's bright Chilean feet.
Rise each dawn to the probing marks
of sanderlings while floating up
from the surf the almost-audible tunes
of murmuring sirens—*bulka, kapusta, shushpie.*
Might ease the final trip to Graveyard Spit,
ashes scattered near sticky daisy, sand verbena,
rocket pea, bill of the pirouetting phalarope.

Afterword

When Two Sylvias Press first approached me about releasing a second edition of *What the Truth Tastes Like*, I was elated beyond measure. Kelli Russell Agodon and Annette Spaulding-Convy, the dynamic duo behind Two Sylvias Press, have released over a dozen impeccably-designed collections, including the first e-anthology of women's poetry, *Fire On Her Tongue, The Daily Poet: Day-By-Day Prompts For Your Writing Practice,* as well as full-length poetry collections by Natasha Kochicheril Moni and Esther Helfgott, among others, and chapbooks authored by Cecilia Woloch and Michelle Peñaloza. I am incredibly honored to be a member of the Two Sylvias family.

The first edition of *What the Truth Tastes Like* appeared in 1999, having won Nightshade Press's William and Kingman Page Poetry Book Award. Although it garnered a healthy amount of attention for a first book from an unknown author, it went out of print in 2010.

What the Truth Tastes Like's poems date back to 1991, when I first enrolled as a non-matriculating auditor in David Wagoner's graduate poetry workshop at the University of Washington. Two years later, I graduated from UW with an MFA and a manuscript that I would continue to hone for the next six years. During the interim period between grad school and its award-winning publication, *What the Truth Tastes Like* underwent a serious amount of editing. Most of what ended up on a cutting-room floor had found its rightful place, but I'd also sheared off several poems that, soon after the book appeared, I wished were between its covers.

For this reason and many others, getting a shot at a "do-over" with Two Sylvias Press has been a dream come true. Thanks to their hard work, welcoming and enthusiastic attitude and exacting editorial skills, the new and improved version of *Truth* contains twenty poems not in the first edition; at least half have never appeared in print. In addition to doubling the length of the original collection, Kelli and Annette have worked diligently to create a souped-up reprise, with new and improved cover, black and white images within the collection, and a greatly improved overall design.

I'm gratefully indebted to them for their combined talents, editorial and design knowhow, and for trusting and believing in my work. Thanks to them, *What the Truth Tastes Like* has undergone a complete transformation, morphing from beater rig to mint-condition Mustang. I invite you to enjoy the smooth ride from Oklahoma to Graveyard Spit, with stops on the moon, Niagara Falls, Rome, and many elsewheres along the way.

Martha Silano
Seattle, Washington, 2015

Martha Silano's books include: *Blue Positive* (Steel Toe Books 2006), *The Little Office of the Immaculate Conception* (winner of the 2010 Saturnalia Books Poetry Prize), and *Reckless Lovely* (Saturnalia Books 2014). She coedited, with Kelli Russell Agodon, *The Daily Poet: Day-By-Day Prompts For Your Writing Practice* (Two Sylvias Press 2013), and her poems have appeared in *Poetry, Orion, Paris Review, American Poetry Review,* and *North American Review,* where she received the 2014 James Hearst Poetry Prize, as well as dozens of anthologies, including *American Poetry: The Next Generation* and *The Best American Poetry 2009.* Martha has been awarded fellowships from the University of Arizona Poetry Center, Washington State Artist Trust, Washington 4Culture, and Seattle Arts Commission, among others. She edits *Crab Creek Review,* curates Beacon Bards, a Seattle-based reading series, and teaches at Bellevue College.

Publications by Two Sylvias Press:

The Daily Poet: Day-By-Day Prompts For Your Writing Practice
by Kelli Russell Agodon and Martha Silano (Print and eBook)

Fire On Her Tongue: An Anthology of Contemporary Women's Poetry
edited by Kelli Russell Agodon and Annette Spaulding-Convy (Print and eBook)

The Poet Tarot and Guidebook: A Deck Of Creative Exploration (Print)

What The Truth Tastes Like
by Martha Silano (Print and eBook)

landscape / heartbreak
by Michelle Peñaloza (Print and eBook)

Earth, Winner of the 2014 Two Sylvias Press Chapbook Prize
by Cecilia Woloch (Print and eBook)

The Cardiologist's Daughter
by Natasha Kochicheril Moni (Print and eBook)

She Returns to the Floating World
by Jeannine Hall Gailey (Print and eBook)

Hourglass Museum
by Kelli Russell Agodon (eBook)

Cloud Pharmacy
by Susan Rich (eBook)

Dear Alzheimer's: A Caregiver's Diary & Poems
by Esther Altshul Helfgott (eBook)

Listening to Mozart: Poems of Alzheimer's
by Esther Altshul Helfgott (eBook)

Crab Creek Review 30th Anniversary Issue featuring Northwest Poets
edited by Kelli Russell Agodon and Annette Spaulding-Convy (eBook)

Please visit Two Sylvias Press (www.twosylviaspress.com) for information on purchasing our print books, eBooks, writing tools, and for submission guidelines for our annual chapbook prize. Two Sylvias Press also offers editing services and manuscript consultations.

Created with the belief that great writing
is good for the world.

two sylvias press

Visit us online: www.twosylviaspress.com

Wishing Well, Sausage Tree, Naranja, Fla.
(20 miles so. of Miami)   388

CPSIA information can be obtained
at www.ICGtesting.com
Printed in the USA
FSOW02n1354130317
31866FS